STANLEY P.S.

KT-134-753

Salmon

Written by Stephen Savage

Illustrated by Colin Newman

Wayland

Ant   Blackbird   Butterfly

Duck   Frog   Oak tree

Rabbit   Salmon   Seagull

Spider

Series editor: Francesca Motisi
Designer: Jean Wheeler

First published in 1995 by
Wayland (Publishers) Ltd
61 Western Road, Hove
East Sussex BN3 1JD, England

© Copyright 1995 Wayland (Publishers) Ltd

British Library Cataloguing in Publication Data

Savage, Stephen
Salmon. - (Observing Nature Series)
I. Title II. Newman, Colin III Series
597.55

ISBN 0-7502-1603-4

Printed and bound in Italy by
G. Canale & C.S.p.A., Turin
Typeset by Jean Wheeler

Contents

What is a salmon?

Salmon are a type of fish that live in many different oceans. Like all fish, they have a tail and fins that they use for swimming. They can breathe under water using gills that are inside their head.

The adult salmon spends most of its life in the sea, but lives in fresh water when it is younger. There are many different types of salmon. This one is called the Atlantic salmon because it lives in the Atlantic Ocean.

Dangers at sea

killer whales

The adult salmon face many dangers in the sea.

They may be attacked and eaten by much larger fish,

or even sharks. Salmon are also hunted and eaten by

killer whales and seals.

Humans are also a danger to salmon. Hundreds of salmon are caught in huge fishing nets for people to eat.

From sea to river

In the spring and summer, adult salmon swim great distances across the sea. They are returning to the river where they hatched. Salmon have a very good sense of smell. They can find the right river because of the smell given off by the rocks, soil and plants.

The adult salmon will swim far up the river. They may have to leap up small waterfalls on the way.

Male and female

The male salmon, who has now changed colour, arrives at the top of the river first. The body of the male salmon has become red and the lower jaw is now hook-shaped.

male

The male salmon attracts a female.

She then chooses the best place to make

a nest and lay her eggs.

female

Making a nest

The female looks for a place where the river
is not too shallow. It must also be a place
where the eggs will not be washed away.
She flicks her tail from side to side until
she has made a nest hole in the tiny
stones at the bottom of the river.

The male and female salmon
lie side by side in the nest
and the female lays her eggs.

Laying the eggs

The female lays several hundred eggs which are soon buried in the gravel. She may not lay all her eggs on the same day. The male and female often find a quiet place to rest and may lay more eggs the next day.

When all the eggs have been laid, the salmon drift slowly back down to the sea. They are tired and hungry as they have not eaten since they left the sea. Some of the adult salmon will die from tiredness or disease.

The eggs

Some of the eggs will be eaten by other animals but most will become hidden in the gravel. The eggs stay at the bottom of the river throughout the winter. Then they hatch in the springtime when the water is warmer.

The newly hatched fish are two centimetres long and are called fry. The salmon fry have a yolk sac which is a special egg food. The fry do not have to catch food for themselves and can hide from danger.

salmon fry

yolk sac

Young salmon

After six weeks, the yolk food has all gone. The salmon fry now leave their hiding places in the gravel to look for food. The young salmon will catch and eat small shrimp-like animals and insect larvae.

heron

The river is full of dangers for the small fish fry. A heron stands in the shallow water ready to grab a fish in its long beak. The kingfisher sits on a branch ready to dive into the water.

kingfisher

Growing up

When the young salmon are nine centimetres long they are called parr. They now have dark patches on their body to help them hide from danger.

They slowly swim down the river towards the sea.

A journey that may take them two years or more.

When they arrive, they will be about sixteen

centimetres long and are called smoult.

The sea

Just before the young salmon reach the sea, they come to the estuary. This is where the river meets the sea. This water is more salty than the river, but not as salty as the sea. The young salmon stay in the estuary for a while to get used to the salty water.

When they are ready, the young salmon will leave the estuary. They will swim far out to sea and continue to grow. It may be another four years before they are ready to return to the river like their parents.

Salmon and people

Many people like to eat salmon. In some parts of the world, salmon are grown in special fish farms. In the winter, the eggs are collected from adult fish living on the farm.

When the eggs hatch, the young fry are fed a special fish food so that they will grow quickly. After one or two years, the young salmon are moved to special sea cages. Here, the salmon grow to a large size and are sold for people to eat.

Other salmon

Some types of salmon live in the Pacific Ocean. The king salmon is the largest type of salmon and may weigh fifty kilogrammes. The smallest type of salmon is the pink salmon. These Pacific salmon also swim up rivers to lay their eggs.

king salmon

Trout are very similar to salmon.
The sea trout migrates up rivers
like a salmon, while the brown
trout spends all its life in
fresh water.

brown trout

pink salmon

Who eats salmon?

Salmon are eaten by many other animals in different parts of the world. In Britain and Europe, salmon are eaten by seals and fish-eating birds. The osprey eats fish, including small adult salmon and trout. It can grab a fish from the water with its clawed feet.

osprey

In America, bald eagles catch live salmon and fish that have died after mating. Grizzly bears can catch salmon by using their teeth and claws.

Life cycle of a salmon

1 What is a salmon?

2 Dangers at sea

3 From sea to river

4 Male and female

5 Making a nest

6 Laying the eggs

7 The eggs

8 Young salmon

9 Growing up

10 The sea

11 Salmon and people

Glossary

estuary The place where a river widens and meets the sea, with a mixing of fresh water and salt water.

fish farms Farms where people breed only fish, including salmon, to sell for food.

gills The parts of a fish's body that allow it to breathe in water.

larvae The grubs that hatch from insects' eggs.

migrates A salmon migrates by returning up river from the sea to the place where it was born, in order to have its young.

Index